In *Faces*, Vita Sackville-West traces the origins and history of forty-four dog breeds. She reflects on their characteristics with frank humour, from the gentle-eyed Afghan, 'like somebody's elderly Aunt Lavinia, who nourishes a secret passion for the Vicar', to the Labrador Retriever, 'dear, solid, faithful lump of a dog!', and that 'docile minion' the Corgi.

Each profile is accompanied by Laelia Goehr's striking black and white photographs. Together, profile and portrait capture these canine characters in their various moods: benevolent, haughty, amused, wistful, or simply a little bit sleepy.

Charming and fascinat'
Faces is a joyful read fo

Faces

Faces

PROFILES OF DOGS

Text by Vita Sackville-West
Photographs by Laelia Goehr

DAUNT BOOKS

This edition first published in the United Kingdom in 2019 by
DAUNT BOOKS
83 Marylebone High Street
London W1U 4QW

2

Copyright © The Beneficiaries of the Estate of
Vita Sackville-West, 1961

Copyright in the Photographs © The Beneficiaries of
the Estate of Laelia Goehr, 1961

First published in Great Britain in 1961 by Harvill Press Limited

A CIP catalogue record for this title is available
from the British Library.

ISBN 978 1 911 54746 4

Typeset by Marsha Swan

Printed and bound by TJ International Ltd, Padstow, Cornwall

www.dauntbookspublishing.co.uk

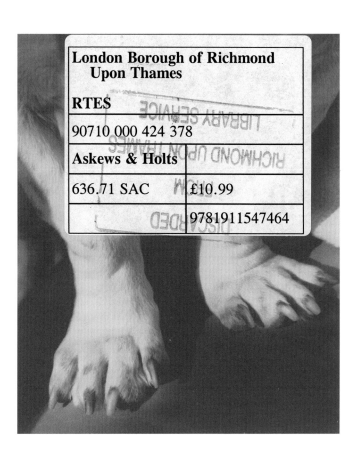

Foreword

'There is in some men a naturall dislike
and abhorring of Cattes, their nature being
so composed that not onely when they see
them, but being neare them and unseen
and hid of purpose, they fall into passions,
fretting, sweating, pulling off their hats and
trembling fearfully . . .'

I would not go so far as that, but I do prefer dogs.

The notes I have appended to Laelia Goehr's magnificent and imaginative illustrations are very amateurish

indeed. I am sure they are full of blunders for which I hope I may be forgiven. All I have tried to do was to give some sort of personal interpretation about the dog under consideration, and I have not hesitated to say whether I disliked or admired the dog I was writing about.

I may thus have given offence to some lovers of lap-dogs or toy-dog breeds, because, as the readers of these notes will readily discover, my taste is for the large, noble, romantic, and aesthetically decorative animal.

Anyhow, the only way I could treat the subjects Laelia Goehr supplied was to look at them with a fresh eye and to find out something about them which might make amusing reading. I have tried to find out little stories and anecdotes about them.

I hope I have not made my notes too anthropomorphic. When one loves dogs, it is difficult not to attribute human qualities to them, so one almost automatically writes 'he' instead of 'it'. One's own dog is not *it*, but *he* or *she*.

How very odd it must be to be a dog, when you come to think of it. He must have crept in, thousands of years ago, to share man's hearth and man's first fire. And now he lies, in his complicated breeds, in our civilised houses, centrally heated; yet he still lies humbly on the floor, waiting for his dinner, and for a loving caress from his owner.

Contents

one | THE BASSET HOUND | 1

two | THE BEDLINGTON TERRIER | 4

three | THE SALUKI OR GAZELLE-HOUND | 8

four | THE BLOODHOUND | 12

five | THE BORZOI | 16

six | THE CHOW | 20

seven | THE COCKER SPANIEL | 24

eight | THE SCHNAUZER | 28

nine | THE DALMATIAN | 32

ten | THE CAVALIER KING CHARLES SPANIEL | 36

eleven | THE DOBERMANN | 40

twelve | THE BULLMASTIFF | 44

thirteen | THE YORKSHIRE TERRIER | 48

fourteen | THE SKYE TERRIER | 52

fifteen | THE PUG | 56

sixteen | THE GREYHOUND | 60

seventeen | THE BOXER | 64

eighteen | THE MINIATURE POODLE | 68

nineteen | THE BEAGLE | 72

twenty | THE AFGHAN HOUND | 76

twenty-one | THE OLD ENGLISH OR
BOBTAIL SHEEPDOG | 80

twenty-two | THE PEKINGESE | 84

twenty-three | THE ALSATIAN | 88

twenty-four | THE IRISH WATER SPANIEL | 92

twenty-five | THE FOXHOUND | 96

twenty-six | THE KERRY BLUE TERRIER | 100

twenty-seven | THE DACHSHUND | 104

twenty-eight | THE ST BERNARD | 108

twenty-nine | THE WHIPPET | 112

thirty | THE IRISH SETTER | 116

thirty-one | THE CORGI | 120

thirty-two | THE CHIHUAHUA | 124

thirty-three | THE BEARDED COLLIE | 128

thirty-four | THE GREAT DANE | 132

thirty-five | THE PAPILLON OR BUTTERFLY-DOG | 136

thirty-six | THE BULLDOG | 140

thirty-seven | THE SHIH TZU | 144

thirty-eight | THE LABRADOR RETRIEVER | 148

thirty-nine | THE MONGREL | 152

forty | THE BASENJI | 156

forty-one | THE COLLIE | 160

forty-two | THE WIRE-HAIRED FOX-TERRIER | 164

forty-three | THE MASTIFF | 168

forty-four | THE SAMOYED | 172

one

THE BASSET HOUND

He stands very low to the ground, which explains his name, for he started life as a Frenchman, *chien courant à jambes courtes.* His legs are indeed very short, though not short enough to make him look like one of those small ottomans one can push about on castors. He is a sporting dog, not a lapdog; and his job is to pursue the hare which as we all know is a very rapidly moving animal.

No one could dislike blood-sports more than I, but one must not extend one's human prejudice to a creature whose instinct impels him to take part in them. If the basset wants to chase a hare, who shall blame him? It is we who have encouraged him to do so. We imported him from France in 1860 or so; and in 1875 the painter Sir John Everett Millais exhibited his French hound Model on the show-bench as a novelty. The English soon discovered his sporting qualities, and within thirty years had him in organised packs – not very many packs, it is true, for even today (1961) there are only about a dozen in the whole country. It has sometimes been asked why we bothered about the basset when we already had the beagle. The answer seems to be that the basset has a finer nose for a catchy scent on cold ploughland; has less tendency to 'flash', i.e. overrun the scent and thereby lose the hare; and that people who appreciate the finer subtleties of hound-work prefer to follow the basset.

Let us leave this clever, stumpy little hound to his professional business, and consider him as a personal companion. In order to do this we must shuffle the show-bench basset and the hare-hunting basset and the private-pet basset into three different categories, for although at least one breeder hunts her dogs as well as showing them, that would not be the ambition of the one-dog man or woman who just wants somebody on four legs to take him or her out for a country walk.

I have never yet owned a basset, but I sometimes think I would very much like to. He would be nice and solid to pat; silky to stroke; and those long leathery ears would be voluptuously and sleepily soft to fondle. Besides, he is said to be affectionate and docile, though the hare's opinion might differ.

And then there is his voice. I started to write a cleri-hew about it:

The basset
Has a great asset.
His deep melodious voice
Makes all but the hare rejoice.

Who would not prefer a bark resembling the deep bass notes of a cello, to the ear-splitting screech of an over-blown trumpet?

two

THE BEDLINGTON
TERRIER

If ever a dog looked like a child's toy, the Bedlington does. In my amateur ignorance I should have described his coat as curly and woolly, but I now discover the technical expression to be *linty*, a charming word which I had never encountered before. It means 'soft like flax or lint', and I thought what an unusual, pretty name it would be for a dog; easy to call. 'Linty! Linty! Linty! Come back at once, Linty.'

Curly and woolly like a lamb, the Bedlington shall, however, remain for me. Yet there is otherwise nothing of the plaything about the Bedlington, a Northumbrian endowed with northern hardiness, swift on the legs, and an enthusiastic rat-catcher. His ancestry is believed to include the far more squat Dandie-Dinmont, a breed which occasionally threw an undesirably long-legged puppy who, if not drowned at birth, might sire or bear similar progeny; it has also been thought that the Bedlington may have something of the lurcher and whippet in him. Whatever the truth, it was not until 1869 that the Bedlington officially received his name and became established in his rights as a distinct form of terrier. Doubtless there had been Bedlingtons before then, but unless we are to accept the story that one Joseph Ainsley, a mason of Bedlington in Northumberland, gave his dog the name of Bedlington in 1825, we must presume that the long-legged Dandie-cum-lurcher-cum-whippet had previously been known as the Northern-Counties-fox-terrier and sometimes as the Rothbury. This name of Rothbury is due to the fact that a Mr Edward Donkin of Flottenbury hunted a pack of foxhounds in the Rothbury district and with them he ran two famous terriers called Peachem and Pincher. Peachem and Pincher were grand little dogs in their day, and in their way, but, as is the way of fashion, they were superseded by something better – in other words by the offspring of Joseph Ainsley's dog Peachem (not the same Peachem, these names are dreadfully confusing) and a bitch called Phoebe, who after three generations of breeding produced Ainsley's Piper, the true begetter of the Bedlington.

They are said to be 'rattling good terriers, active and alert, but distinctly pugnacious in their constant desire to tear each other'. One has to translate this jargon into plain English, and in plain English I should say that 'distinctly pugnacious' meant that they were terrible fighters. Never having known a Bedlington in any degree of intimacy, I can't tell whether this indictment is deserved or libellous, so do not let me take his character away. All I can say is that his wooden appearance does not much appeal to me, however linty his coat may be.

three

THE SALUKI OR GAZELLE-HOUND

The Saluki is an Arab; in fact, *saluk* in Arabic means hound, and it is further suggested, with some plausibility, that the breed originated in the town or district of Saluk. Possibly the oldest breed in the world, their portrait appears in mural paintings in Egyptian tombs, notably in the tomb of Rechmara, 1400 BC. This, and the fact that they were also known in Persia and China, despite the reluctance of the Arabs to part with their dogs, implies that they were greatly valued for their swiftness and endurance in hunting and formed an acceptable present to the princes of those distant lands.

'Oh my Huntsman,' writes a Persian poet in AD 800, 'bring me my dogs brought by the Kings of Saluk,' and remarked further that a Saluki ran so fast that his feet and his head seemed joined in his collar, which is scarcely surprising when we reflect that they were used in the pursuit of gazelle, antelope, and hare. If the cheetah is the swiftest animal on earth, the Saluki must run it very close.

They enjoyed also the honour of being modelled by Benvenuto Cellini for Cosimo dei Medici.

These most romantic of dogs were practically unknown in England before the end of the nineteenth century. A Mr Allen, in the 1880s, had exhibited one Jierma, whose unusual grace aroused much excitement and caused her to be mistakenly described as a Persian greyhound. But it was not until after 1895, when the Hon. Florence Amherst was presented with two puppies bred by sheikhs of a Bedouin tribe, that the breed became established here and caught the popular imagination to such an extent that some exhibitors 'added an Eastern glamour to the proceedings by appearing in full native dress'.

Salukis resemble their native desert in colouring, as any traveller familiar with the desert under varying lights will agree. They may be a plain pale tan, or grizzled, or golden, or cream or even white as some of the sand-dunes. The lovely creature in the photograph displays the silky ears, and undoubtedly possesses also 'feathers' of the same texture down the back of the legs and on the curly tail. There are also smooth-coated Salukis with no feathers, to my mind less attractive.

I once had a Saluki, presented to me in Baghdad straight out of the desert by Miss Gertrude Bell, without exception the dullest dog I ever owned. Salukis are reputed to be very gentle and faithful; this one, Zurcba, meaning the yellow one, was gentle enough because she was completely spiritless, and as for fidelity she was faithful only to the best armchair. I took her up from Baghdad into Persia, where nothing would induce her to come out for a walk – perhaps because I omitted to provide a gazelle. In the end I followed the historical tradition and gave her to a Persian prince, who subsequently lost her somewhere in Moscow. I was unlucky, of course, in the only Saluki I ever owned, and these remarks must not be taken as an aspersion upon an incomparably elegant and ancient race.

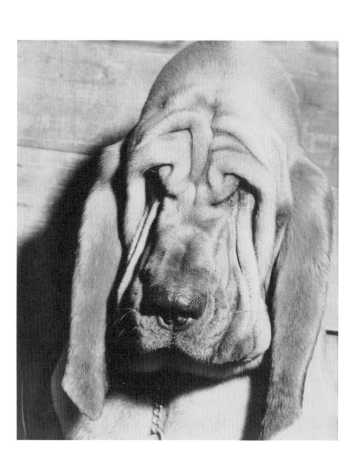

four

THE BLOODHOUND

Hard to believe that this benevolent and somnolent gentleman should be the terror of fugitive criminals. Despite his name, his appearance suggests no more ferocity than the grumpiness of a confirmed old clubman on finding his favourite armchair occupied by a new member.

The name is indeed misleading. No one should be undeservedly saddled with a name implying a pugnacious or sanguinary disposition. In private life the bloodhound, rightly described as noble, dignified, solemn and wise, lives up to his suggestion of the ideal grandpapa who would secretly slip a gold coin, when such things existed, into the expectant palm of the schoolboy at the end of the holidays.

Human grandpapas presumably have their share of personal cares unsuspected by the schoolboy, but what about those worried wrinkles on the face of the bloodhound? Has he his troubles too? So long ago as 1607 it was observed by the Reverend Edward Topsell that 'they wring their faces and draw their skins through overmuch intention (like sorrowful persons)'. Unbearable though the thought of a sorrowful bloodhound may be, we can well believe that over much intention has crumpled throughout the centuries the faces of a conscientious race endowed by Nature with a particularly responsible kind of Nose. It enjoined almost a moral obligation on its owner: the obligation to make the best possible use of it in the service of man the master. Man the master, all-wise and presumably omnipotent, might on occasion stand in need of protection. It sometimes happened that he was attacked, robbed, even murdered; his house broken into, his wife strangled, his children kidnapped and nowhere to be found. Man had many resources: dozens of dark-blue policemen arrived at his command, but there was something that he and his policemen lacked: the Nose.

The Nose was the thing. Not in vain was the breed associated with the sleuth-hounds of Scotland in 1575, credited with 'a marvellous wit', able to discover the whereabouts of miscreants after they had fled.

The miscreants had not much to fear. Bloodhounds are used on the trail because of their exceptional power of scent and their determination never to desist until they have run down their quarry, but having run him down they do not proceed to devour him. It is related that in the West Indies bloodhounds were employed in chasing escaped slaves in the cruel hope of seeing the victim pulled down and torn to pieces. This hope proved so vain that men out of work in Florida would offer themselves in return for a small payment to be hunted by a whole pack.

No. The name is indeed misleading, for it really denotes blue blood in the most aristocratic sense of the word. They came to England with the Normans at the time of the Conquest, and it is believed that one of the breed landed on English soil with William the Conqueror himself.

There are few families who can boast of so long a pedigree.

five

THE BORZOI

Elegant beyond any question, with that long lean head and graceful attitude. These are truly princely dogs, for they were bred by the Czars of Russia and the Russian nobility for wolf-coursing, a dangerous sport demanding speed, and courage, and training, as we can well believe when we learn that a couple had to race the wolf, catch it close to the ears, bring it to the ground, and hold it until the horsemen galloped up and secured it. On no account must they let go, or, as we can imagine, they would get severely bitten.

Even if the Czars did not indulge to any great extent personally in the sport, they were proud of their kennels, which in the time of Nicholas II numbered forty to sixty Borzois, not counting puppies, and fourteen men to look after them. This unhappy Czar presented the Princess of Wales (later Queen Alexandra) with the famous champion Alex in 1895, but some thirty years earlier Borzois under the name of Russian or Siberian wolf-hounds had been exhibited by such patrician owners as the Prince of Wales and the Duchess of Manchester; moreover they attained additional fame through being painted by Landseer.

The Russians had a theory that the Borzoi had reached them from Arabia via Mongolia, whence they had travelled in the camps of the Tartar invaders. It seems a far cry and a cork-screwing sort of route, but nothing is impossible when one remembers the extraordinary mobility of warlike hordes over vast areas and of merchant caravans along the great trade-routes of Asia. There appear to have been two types, the Siberian and the Circassian, the latter with a smooth coat instead of a wavy, rather longer legs, a shorter head, and a reputation for a superior intelligence. I suspect that the superior intelligence would be no disadvantage, for I cannot believe that that narrow, elongated head, looking as though it had been trod on by an elephant and flattened, can possibly contain much grey matter. Owing to their Imperial and aristocratic segregation, the Borzoi on his importation into England was found to have become so inbred that it was advisable to strengthen the breed by introducing some deerhound blood.

There is one aspect of the Borzoi, however, which cannot incur the charge of degeneracy, and perhaps prospective owners ought to be warned in case they may get an embarrassing surprise one morning on finding that their Borzoi bitch has given birth to eighteen puppies. It is not unknown, though it may be fair to add that ten or twelve is the more usual number.

six

THE CHOW

No need to scowl: we will neither eat your flesh nor flay your coat as fur. Such was once the practice in China, where the poorer classes ate the adult dogs and the tenderer puppies were reserved for the wealthy. Mr Ash plausibly suggests that this implies a foreign origin for the Chow, since by law a Prince was bidden to value all indigenous things and was forbidden 'to keep even dogs and horses not native to his country'. It would thus follow that if the Chow were in fact the result of a cross between the Siberian Samoyed and the Tibetan mastiff, he could not be regarded as a genuine native of China, and might legitimately take his place among the edible joints hanging up in the butcher's shop. Gilbert White in his *Natural History of Selborne* recounts that he saw a dog and a bitch brought back from Canton by a young gentleman in the service of the East India Company, of a breed 'fattened in that country for the purpose of being eaten'. They were, he says, about the size of a moderate (*sic*) spaniel, of a pale yellow colour, and a very fox-like appearance, with a surly savage demeanour and a bark 'in a short thick manner, like foxes'. This pair, taken on board as soon as weaned, were puzzled, poor puppies, by the diet offered them on arrival in England. Having doubtless inherited a taste for rice-meal and other fattening farinaceous food, they 'did not relish flesh' to start with. Perhaps they retained some atavistic memory of the joints of their uncles, aunts, and cousins dangling from hooks in the back-streets of Canton . . .

They did, however, accept with much greediness the bones of partridges, 'and licked the platter clean'.

The characteristic scowl has remained on that blunt face, as though the Chow preserved a grievance against life. He may also resent his not very complimentary name, for Chow-chow in pidgin English means any odd variety of assorted merchandise, and as such was he listed on the ship which first brought him to England in 1780. But how to account for the blue-black tongue, gums, and roof of the mouth, which occur in no other dogs all the world over? I suppose there must be some explanation of this freak of pigmentation, but if there is I do not know it. How to account for the peculiarly stilted gait, due to the inflexible stiffness of the hind legs? Gilbert White noticed it: an awkward gait, he calls it, when they trot, without any bend at the hock or ham. Gilbert White was an observant man, and owners of Chows will confirm his remarks as still applicable today.

seven

THE COCKER SPANIEL

It is not surprising that this silky little creature should be so popular, for it combines sporting instincts in the field with domestic affection in the house, and as a puppy is irresistible. It would seem also that, the sporting instincts denied their scope, it can accommodate itself with the utmost resignation to an uneventful existence. No dog ever led a duller or more sedentary life than Miss Elizabeth Barrett's Flush, whose ears so closely resembled his mistress's curls.

And yet the very name *cocker* was specially applied to a spaniel small enough to penetrate the thick undergrowth where woodcock crouched concealed, and in the reign of Queen Elizabeth I was used to drive game and birds into nets. They are active little dogs, with nothing nambypamby about them, in spite of a loving nature amounting to sentimentality. Their colour, according to taste, may be red, golden, tan, blue roan, black or black and white, so there is plenty of variety to choose from.

It is thought that the spaniel originated in Spain, and in the beginning of their recorded history, which goes back to 1387, they were all generically known as spaniels. It was not until 1790 that they began to be divided into separate varieties. After that we get so many types that the amateur may be forgiven for a failure to disentangle them. There is the English Springer, the Clumber, the Sussex, the Welsh Springer, the Irish Water and the Field Spaniel, which is really a larger version of the Cocker. The main difference seems to lie in the size and weight; the Field may weigh anything from 35 lb to 50 lb, the little Cocker should not exceed 28.

The solemn face in the illustration gives no idea of the cheerful disposition of one that is nicknamed the Merry Cocker. I believe also that they have a sense of humour; some dogs have. I once owned a golden cocker bitch and a cream Persian cat; the spaniel had puppies and the cat kittens at the same time, puppies and kittens being of exactly the same colour. The spaniel used to steal the kittens and deposit them amongst her own offspring, suckling them all indiscriminately, and I would swear that the little dog grinned up at me whenever I went to sort them out. I should add that the cat in her turn stole the puppies, but I was never able to discern the slightest trace of amusement on her face.

eight

THE SCHNAUZER

It must be a nuisance to go through life with a Father Christmas moustache like that, but no doubt the Schnauzer gets used to it. These dogs are not often seen in this country, though a smaller edition, the miniature Schnauzer, has recently begun to find favour.

The only Schnauzer I ever knew, a descendant of the prize-winning Egelsee strain which not unnaturally caused him to be known as Mr Egg, spent most of his time lying in the middle of a village street, watching the traffic go by, and how he escaped being run over passes my comprehension. Yet they are said to be home-loving and good guard dogs, besides having a particular aptitude for catching and destroying venomous snakes.

Their country of origin is Germany, especially in the south, where they act as sheepdogs in the mountainous regions on the German–Austrian border. Their name is rather an unkind one, for *Schnauze* is the equivalent of our word snout, but at various times they have more politely been called *Rauche* (rough-haired) Pinschers, with the qualification *Rattfänger* (rat-catchers) added in brackets. They are very square-looking dogs, particularly when the beard and moustache have been trimmed, and they have bushy eyebrows which would arouse the envy of any colonel. In England, fortunately, the cropping of ears is illegal, so the Schnauzer is allowed to retain his dropping ears intact instead of being condemned to having them truncated, and the stumps trained to stand upright. His tail is docked, but, as everybody knows, that operation entails no suffering upon a newly born puppy.

Taken all in all, with the exception of the ears, this German dog bears a certain resemblance to the Airedale terrier, especially in Germany and Austria where they are bred to stand higher on the leg than here. But the Airedale is black and tan and the Schnauzer is pepper and salt, though black is permissible but rare. Mr Egg regrettably, in spite of his aristocratic descent, was pewter-grey, which would have lost him as many marks on the show-bench as had he been sandy or even red. I don't suppose Mr Egg gave a hoot to his colouring, any more than he took any notice of the lorries that swerved to avoid him.

He was an arrogant dog.

nine

THE DALMATIAN

Oddly enough, the Dalmatian does not come from Dalmatia. He more likely comes from Italy, though he has also been suggested as an Indian dog and certainly bears a resemblance to the spotted Bengal harrier. An additional reason for believing him to be an Italian, is that in Cromwellian times in England when the Roman Catholic Church was more than usually unpopular, members of that Church were portrayed on broadsheets and handbills accompanied by a Dalmatian. How, then, to explain the name? One theory, which may seem rather far-fetched, is that some rocks in Dalmatia are pitted in such a way as to remind travellers of dogs they had seen elsewhere, and the nickname stuck. To us, its other nicknames of plum-pudding dog or carriage-dog are familiar.

The poor carriage-dog has outlived his function. No longer does he trot sedately along the lanes under the gig or pony-cart on those straight untireable legs and rough tough pads specially adapted to gravel. He cannot keep up with the motor-car. Yet he should not be discarded on that account. He is still as good a guard-dog as in the days when his deep baying voice was relied on to scare the footpads, nor could you have a cleaner dog or one that brings less mud into the house. Moreover he can be trained as a gundog, when over a long day's shooting his qualities of endurance will come into play. He is not so large as the Great Dane, to whom he may be related, his weight being a mere 55 lb or so compared with the Dane's 120, another advantage because it means that he does not eat so much. Yes, a nice dog, the Dalmatian; not so handsome as some, perhaps, and lacking the Dane's majestic dignity, also slightly comic because of his plum-pudding sobriquet and his association with the circus. The name is not his fault, and personally I have never been able to see any likeness between our brown Christmas pudding and a dog whose groundwork is invariably white. Perhaps the suet-roll studded with raisins is the pudding meant.

By the way, should you breed from a Dalmatian bitch, do not be alarmed if the puppies, or some of them, are born pure white. The spots will develop within a few weeks' time. But of course if you are going in for breeding, you will know this already.

ten

THE CAVALIER KING
CHARLES SPANIEL

There is a legend, which surely should be capable of either proof or disproof, that in the reign of King Charles I an edict was issued granting the toy spaniels admission 'to any establishment in the kingdom'. The Lord Chamberlain's Office disclaims all knowledge of such an edict; the King Charles Spaniel Club says that although nobody can prove that it has ever been repealed, nobody can prove that it never existed either. The legal authorities at the House of Commons are equally unhelpful. It seems unlikely therefore that this winning little face has no right of entry into establishments where dogs are not welcome.

In any case, an edict of Charles I could scarcely apply to the King Charles or his relations, since the original King Charles was first brought over from France by Charles II's sister, the beloved and unfortunate Minette, Henrietta Duchess of Orleans. It is of course possible that some law applied to an earlier type, known as the Spanish-Gentle, or Comforter, which in the reign of Queen Elizabeth I was believed to give relief from pain and fever if hugged against the stomach, rather like a living hot-water bottle. Whatever the truth, the toy spaniel rapidly found favour in royal and aristocratic circles. King Charles, like Cavaliers, have the same colour variants: the true King Charles, or Black-and-Tan; the Ruby, a chestnut-red; the Tricolours, sometimes called Prince Charles, white with black patches and tan markings; and the Blenheim, white with chestnut patches, possibly a cross made for the Duke of Marlborough between a King Charles and a red and white cocker. But King Charles all have squashed noses and domed foreheads, and to my mind are far less attractive than the Cavalier King Charles in the illustration.

Cavalier is a fancy name and has nothing whatsoever to do with Charles I as might be supposed, although spaniels like him may be seen in pictures by Van Dyck and contemporary Dutch painters. He owes his present existence to a prize offered by an American gentleman, Mr Roswell Eldridge, for a spaniel with a long nose and no dome to the skull. It was thus only in 1928 that the Cavalier King Charles Club was founded, and it is satisfactory to record that the Kennel Club registrations by 1960 numbered over eleven hundred, nearly one thousand in excess of the crumpled-faced King Charles.

One cannot help wondering to what sort of spaniel the following advertisement referred: 'The Marchesa Siffanti di San Bartolomeo is in want of a young healthy wet-nurse. Her services will be required for a litter of five English spaniels thoroughbred, the maternal parent having died. Nurse to reside in the house; wages 100 francs a month; chocolate in the morning; breakfast with the Marchesa; dine with the servants; sleep with the dogs.'

eleven

THE DOBERMANN

The Hound of the Baskervilles effect so brilliantly achieved in the illustration is somewhat misleading, for Herr Dobermann's dog is sleek and rather snaky and built on greyhound lines. On the other hand, the ferocious aspect caught by the camera may not be so misleading after all, or may be the one most familiar to miscreants in Palestine where they are (or once were) favourite tracker-dogs of the police.

The Dobermann was known until quite lately as the Dobermann Pinscher, which gave him a false reputation as he is not in the least like a terrier. The truth is that

Herr Dobermann was a dog catcher and no one, not even Herr Dobermann, knew the exact antecedents of his dog.

There are several different kinds of Pinscher: the Harlequin, the Wire-haired, the Smooth-haired which resembles a Boxer especially when his tail has been docked and his ears cropped and rounded (forbidden in this country), the miniature or Reh Pinscher, and the diminutive Affenpinscher, or monkey-terrier, which probably entered at some time into the ancestry of the Brussels Griffon. There was a theory that Herr Dobermann, who lived at Apolda in Thuringia, created the dog which bears his name by crossing the German Pinscher with the Alsatian; the black-and-brown colouring of the Alsatian has been inherited, but not the deep fur, Herr Dobermann's dog being of a satiny texture. Rust-red markings stain the coat on the muzzle, throat, chest, legs and feet, and below the tail. I met two of them in Rio de Janeiro, and thought them decorative as well as amiable. Occasionally in provincial France you may encounter a dog easily mistaken for a Dobermann, but he is much more likely to be a Beauce sheepdog, so called from the region of La Beauce.

The Dobermann is much liked in America, where I understand he rivals the Boston terrier in popularity and yet the Boston terrier is known over there as the National dog of the United States.

twelve

THE BULLMASTIFF

That wrinkled forehead and those tearful eyes make him look wistful in the photograph, but you should see him standing four-square, jaw well advanced, determination written all over him. Believe it or not, you will find him twice as heavy to lift as the bulldog, should you feel bold enough to try the experiment. The bulldog, whom most of us probably think of as a lump of solidity, turns the scales at a mere 50 to 55 lb compared with the Bullmastiff's 120 to 130. The true mastiff beats them both at 150.

These are the two breeds which have given rise to the Bullmastiff. It seems so natural to have intercrossed the two, that the Bullmastiff may well have existed long before he was given official recognition under his own name by the Kennel Club in 1925. Gamekeepers may have loved, and poachers hated, him, but he was scarcely designed to be everybody's pet, and thus probably remained in the obscurity of the woods, the companion of men on either their lawful or their lawless occasions. He is said to be sometimes favoured with a gentle and affectionate disposition, sometimes not; all I can say is that I should hesitate to pat him, in case it was the sometimes not.

It may interest picture-lovers to know that the dog in the foreground of Velasquez's *Las meniñas* is a Castilian mastiff. I made the acquaintance of one in Madrid, a most courteous animal who might have walked straight out of Velasquez's canvas and whom I greatly coveted. Unfortunately or perhaps fortunately he already belonged to a film-star, and was not for me.

One may presume that the mastiff who accompanied Don Garcia de Figueroa on his embassy to Shah Abbas in Persia in the early years of the seventeenth century was of this Castilian breed. It is on record that this dog, confronted with a bas-relief carving of a mastiff on the ruins of Persepolis, furiously attacked his semblance in stone – a pleasing anecdote which to my mind does not carry conviction. It is claimed in support of its authenticity that the smooth grey stone of Persepolis was polished as highly as the surface of a mirror, thus deluding the dog into a belief in his own reflection. This must be sheer, though pretty, nonsense. Everyone knows that a puppy may be taken in the first time it catches sight of itself in a mirror, and may fling itself against the rival, but when once it has badly bumped its nose it will have got wise to the deception.

The Bullmastiff refused to sit for our artist.
Inquirers referred to portrait of his ancestor by Velasquez.

I do wish I could believe the story of the living Spanish mastiff attacking the stone mastiff of Darius, immobilised and immortalised two thousand years before.

thirteen

THE YORKSHIRE TERRIER

One would have to be born with a very odalisque nature to enjoy being a show Yorkshire terrier. One might find oneself lying on a silk cushion inside a glass case, and that would be the least of the indignities to which one was subjected. One might be kept in a box, except for brief intervals when one was let out for some gentle play and natural purposes – about the only natural thing in this highly artificial existence. Above all, one must not run any risk of damaging one's appearance, and to this end one would have one's top-knot plaited and tied up with a ribbon to keep it out of harm's way.

One would wear chamois-leather socks to prevent one from the pleasurable occupation of scratching. One would be provided with several pairs of these socks, as they must be frequently washed and kept scrupulously clean. One's lovely steel-blue coat would be brushed daily – brushed not combed, lest the comb should break the hair – and it would be carefully parted all along the back, to hang down either side. One might have a mixture of paraffin and camphorated oil rubbed into it, to improve the growth and condition, though one's sensitive nose would doubtless prefer Chanel No. 5. As to one's food, it would be strictly regulated – no fat, no bones – and one might even be spoon-fed to safeguard one's mouth from getting messy, or, if one were allowed the independence of eating one's dinner from a dish, one might have a sort of protective mask arranged over one's face. In any case, one would not want very much dinner, for one would be very tiny; and might, if very well-bred indeed, weigh under two lb.

Such a mode of life could have only two effects upon one's outlook: either one would become impotently and fretfully cross, or else one would regard oneself as a sort of superior being, accepting all the slavish ministrations as one's due, but with a certain disdain for the ministrator.

It is not surprising to learn that the Skye terrier and the Maltese both played a part in the making of the Yorkshire. It is more surprising to hear of one who took part with distinction in rat-catching competitions, and slightly surprising to learn also that towards the end of the nineteenth century they became the favourites of working-class men – heavy hands, surely, to manipulate such mites. This reminds us of the Durham miners who cultivated auriculas, perhaps in the same unconscious desire for an escape from a coarse grimy life. We may be sure that they handled their plants and their midget dogs with equal tenderness.

fourteen

THE SKYE TERRIER

With all the love and respect due to the superb island of Skye, I cannot feel that its eponymous terrier is aesthetically worthy of it. Skye may Breed Bonny Bairns; it has also bred a comic rather than a bonny dog, and one most ill-adapted to its native heath. How does it manage that coat, trailing almost to the ground, as it scrambles through tufts of heather taller than itself, or splashes in swamps between the burns? How can it even see the Cuillins, or avoid falling into Loch Scavaig, when its eyes are completely veiled by a fringe of hair?

Somebody must have parted the hair on purpose, to show the bright eyes in the photograph.

The parting of the coat all along the back is *de rigueur*, like the traditional curate. It has the effect of making the dog look as though a rug has been thrown over him, for it hangs down on either side, straight as string, almost concealing the stumpy paws. No wonder the Skye terrier created a sensation when he first appeared in London. There is a delightful story of a certain Mr Pratt, who in 1883 kept a pack of six he was in the habit of exercising in Hyde Park. One day they all tore off in sudden excitement until they came to a drain where they started digging without apparent cause, but later were fully justified, for a badger of all unlikely denizens was discovered down the drain. It is suggestive that Skye terriers were used for driving otters out of their holts between the rocks of their native island, for they are gallant out of all proportion to their size, undeterred by the savage bite of the otter in defence of his life. In fact they will take on any small animal they regard as vermin, be it otter, badger, rat or weasel, and in default of legitimate prey will even turn with murderous intent upon each other.

The story of Mr Pratt and his dogs has a sequel. Two years after the badger incident, he received a letter from

Norway, addressed The Man with the Dogs, Paddington, London, the envelope being illustrated by a sketch of Mr Pratt and his six terriers strung out in a line, with, for good measure, in the background a lady carrying a parasol walking beside a gentleman in a top-hat.

It speaks well for the remarkable appearance of the Skye terriers and also for the resourcefulness of the British Post Office, that the letter should have been duly and promptly delivered.

fifteen

THE PUG

To be honest, I do not like pugs. I cannot abide the snuffle, nor do I care for faces that look as though they had collided with a wall at speed. This personal distaste, however, should not admit prejudice against a breed which some people find attractive, and whose name at one time could be bestowed on a favourite person: he, or she, is my pug. I doubt if it would be taken as a compliment today.

What woman, though, could resist a love-letter beginning: 'My sweete pugge, thy absens will make the returne of thy swete companie the more welcum to me.'

This occurs in a letter dated 1580, in the charters of Berkeley Castle.

The Dutch had no hesitation in adopting the pug as a national hero after the Prince of Orange's dog had awakened him by jumping on to his face and thus saving him from a surprise capture by his enemies. It was even thought that the Dutch were responsible for producing the ugly little creature, by breeding a form of dwarf mastiff, and so much credence did this theory obtain that the pug sometimes became known as the Dutch mastiff. It seems more probable that their country of origin was China, and certainly an innovation in the form of coal-black pugs was introduced from there in the 1880s.

The periods of favour enjoyed by the pug in England show a graph of ups and downs like a temperature chart. From the time of Charles II onwards until the closing years of the eighteenth century he was the fashionable pet both in England and Italy, where he could be seen wearing a neat jacket and trousers, but by the beginning of the nineteenth century only a few samples remained in England. Then came a fresh burst of popularity, when owing to their rarity the available puppies sold for high prices, and ladies of fashion tricked out their pets with necklaces of turquoise and other semi-precious stones. Pugs were considered as especially suitable companions for ladies, owing to their sensitive and nervous disposition; one of them, indeed, was said to have died of fright on seeing a tramp looking at it through the window. Ladies swooned readily in these Victorian days, or so we are told, and so perhaps their pets tactfully swooned with them.

sixteen

THE GREYHOUND

To my shame be it said that I have never yet been to 'the dogs', or not nearer than the television screen. Paul Morand once wrote a brilliantly evocative description of green grass under arc-lights, stream-lined hounds stretched out to the full, and the roaring red-faced audience of the sporting world. It must be a fine sight. Perhaps I have been put off by a suspicion of some essential stupidity in an animal that is content repeatedly to pursue an electric dummy he can't catch, and wouldn't be worth catching if he could. Activated robots; no more; deflected from their original calling of coursing the live hare over the open downs or the deer over the moors. Any intelligent greyhound, released from a box and offered a bogus quarry, would surely sit down on his haunches and sulk.

But beautiful and historical – oh yes, every time. He is Assyrian, Egyptian, Persian, Greek, Roman. He appears in carvings, and on coins, pottery, and cameos. He turns up in England, where in the reign of King Canute 'no mean person may own a greyhound'. Chaucer mentions him as being 'swift as a fowl'. Wynkyn de Worde, Caxton's contemporary, takes him as his device. Dame Juliana Berners of Norwich, that strange shadowy figure of the early fifteenth century, gives a description which she must have observed from the life: 'A Greyhound should be headed like a Snake and necked like a Drake. Footed like a Cat. Tailed like a Rat.' Gervase Markham, a couple of centuries later, says that 'of all dogs whatsoever, he is the most princely, strong, nimble, swift, and valiant'.

He thus has a long tradition behind him, and besides that is related to all the most romantic dogs in the world: the Saluki, the Afghan hound, the Borzoi, the deer-hound, the wolf-hound, as well as to the Great Dane and to that shivering little misery the Italian greyhound, who so caught the fancy of Lobengula King of the Matabele that he gave two hundred head of cattle in exchange for one.

It seems a pity that Markham's 'princely, nimble, swift and valiant' dog should now have been dragged down to the ignominy of being cooped up in a box and released only in pursuit of a silly stuffed hare.

seventeen

THE BOXER

I should not like to say anything in disparagement of the Boxer, because the few that I have met have always seemed most engaging with their funny faces that look as though they were made of india rubber to be pulled in any direction, but honesty compels an admission of rumours of a certain fierceness not desirable in a dog weighing between four and five stone. The advocates of any particular breed have a way of putting these things with a delicate euphemism: 'Any indication of a temperamental tendency to show ill-temper should be sternly discouraged; it (the Boxer) should carry itself with calm self-assurance and the frown on its face is no more than a warning to pay regard to its self-respect.'

Friends assure me that the frown on the face means nothing sinister, and that no dog is gentler or more reliable with children, but in spite of this I shall certainly continue to pay every possible regard to his self-respect.

The Boxer has not long been with us. He was first shown at Munich in 1895 when there were only four entries, the result of a German breeder's ambition to create a smaller version of the British bulldog, with such success that now over seven thousand Boxers a year are registered in England. His parentage includes the Brabant bull-baiter and a hunting hound from the Low Countries, with a dash of our own bulldog, and a small admixture of Great Dane. (These canine pedigrees sometimes read like a cookery recipe.) The Brabant bull-baiter is perhaps unkindly named, as he was used for penning wild cattle rather than for the revolting sport I have, with restraint, described in the note on the bulldog, though doubtless he could also be turned on at times to gratify the strangely persistent blood-lust of man.

The bulldog element shows strongly in the stop, which is the technical term for that depression between the forehead and the nose. Owing to some foreshortening of focus, it is not very apparent in the photograph, but most pronounced in real life. In a less dignified dog, such as the pug, you might think it a ledge specially provided for the balancing of a lump of sugar; not so in this descendant of essentially virile and muscular ancestors.

eighteen

THE MINIATURE POODLE

The miniature poodle suggests to me rows of smart women sitting under driers at a fashionable hairdresser. The dogs, secured by a lead to the leg of their owner's chair, yap and tug and try to get at one another. From time to time an owner says: 'Hush, Tiny darling,' to which Tiny pays no attention whatsoever.

The one in the illustration opposite looks unusually untidy, but a glance at the frontispiece will show what a truly *de luxe* miniature ought to look like. It is not difficult to believe that fashion once allowed a lady's initials to be clipped out on the dog's back, or a heart or a crest

– though this, of course, applied to the larger variety of the breed. Clipping, as a matter of fact, probably originated from the practical necessity of removing some of the heavy coat when poodles were used as water-dogs in Germany, France, and England.

The standard poodle got his name from the German *Pudelhund, puddeln* meaning to splash in Low German, from which derivation we can easily see our own words paddle and puddle.

The large or standard poodle has declined in popularity, while the miniature has soared. One wonders where the diminution will stop.

In justice to these little clowns it must be said that they are not the idiots their owners often try to make them appear. On the contrary, they are amongst the most intelligent of dogs, and if you like a dog that will die for his country or sit up balancing a lump of sugar on his nose, then the poodle is the dog for you. Perhaps such nonsense is more acceptable from poodles than from some other breeds, for whatever merits may be claimed for miniature poodles, dignity is not amongst them. Comic they are, even to their name. One cannot take them seriously, and to my mind a dog that cannot be taken seriously is not a dog at all.

Still, they obviously have their charm, with their ridiculous tufts and their delicately prinking feet. And one must admit that they make an elegant accompaniment to an elegant woman – a sort of accessory like her handbag or her compactum or her make-up and her stiletto heels.

nineteen

THE BEAGLE

'The beagle 'ee ' unts 'ares and the basset 'ee 'unts 'ares
and the 'arrier 'ee 'unts 'ares too but if you want to 'unt
'ares with 'arriers you 'ave to foller 'em on a norse and it
isn't all of us as 'ave got 'orses nor even a pony nowadays
so if you want to 'unt 'ares you'll go out with a pack of
beagles or bassets on your own pair of legs and leave the
'arriers to them as 'ave got 'orses to ride.'

Such was the advice given me by an old countryman.
He little knew how remote was my desire to hunt hares
whether with beagles, bassets or harriers, but he meant
well, doing his best to instruct me in my ignorance.

The beagle has been with us for many years. The 'pocket' beagle, meaning a hound standing under 10 inches in height, appears in history as favoured by Queen Elizabeth I. The name beagle is an odd word of obscure derivation and nobody seems to know what it comes from. In France, they call these hounds *bigle*, but that must surely be a corruption of our English word beagle, since *bigle* in French means squint-eyed and nobody could accuse a beagle of being that.

The beagle stands taller than the basset, and looks more like a small edition of the foxhound. Somehow, I can't take to the beagle as I do to the basset, by which I mean that I don't in the least covet a beagle as a personal companion, as I do rather covet a basset. One can't explain these things. It is just that way, and if one is writing about dogs or about anything else for that matter, one must express what one feels or else what one writes becomes flat and meaningless and without any more life or colour to it than a telephone directory. Perhaps if, like Queen Elizabeth I, I could have a 'pocket' beagle, I might get quite fond of it. Otherwise, no. Let 'em 'unt 'ares to their 'earts' content, so long as I never hear again the scream of a hare like a murdered child.

twenty

THE AFGHAN HOUND

I cannot get it out of my head that the dog in the photograph is like somebody's elderly spinster aunt. A little untidy, perhaps, and badly in need of a hair-trim, but how gentle the eyes are, and the whole expression pleading for affection. A sweet old lady, providing crumpets for tea. Aunt Lavinia, who nourishes a secret passion for the Vicar.

One needs to envisage the whole animal, standing 2 feet 6 inches, silky-shaggy from head to tail, and wearing hairy trousers something like a cowboy's chaps. The Afghans like to think that their dogs are indigenous, and of such antiquity that Noah took a couple into the Ark, but it seems more probable that the Arabian Saluki found its way to Afghanistan and that in the rigorous climate of that high mountainous land it developed the more protective coat.

Just as the Saluki is used for hunting gazelle, so is the Afghan used in the pursuit of small deer, often in company of a hawk. It is even claimed for one of them that he tackled and killed a leopard. Swift and fearless when engaged in this his hereditary business, in private life away from his native home he is said to be shy, and it is endearingly suggested that this timidity may be due to his inability to understand the conditions under which we live. Small blame to him. There must, indeed, be a great difference between an English kennel or even an English garden, and the wild freedom of Central Asian hills.

His powers of endurance are well adapted to the life he is called upon to lead. A Mrs M. Amps, who had kennels at Kabul, described how on trekking twenty to thirty miles daily at altitudes rising to 17,000 feet on the way to Lesser Tibet, her dogs at the end of a long day would think nothing of dashing up the mountainside after marmots.

The Afghan has not long been in England, being exhibited for the first time in 1910 at Crufts, not even accorded the compliment of a name to himself, but relegated to the 'foreign and other variety' class. Zardin, the dog then shown, not unnaturally created a sensation, for nothing like him had ever been seen before. Even today, when we have more or less become accustomed to his extraordinary appearance, he is apt to look startlingly like a dog in a dream. Not in the very least like Aunt Lavinia.

twenty-one

THE OLD ENGLISH OR BOBTAIL SHEEPDOG

Who so hard-hearted as to resist the nose and paws in the illustration? The subject is obviously a darling. What does it matter if he appears to have no eyes, except that we must wonder how he manages to see his way through life? The trouble about him, considered as a household pet, is his coat; technically described among breeders as 'profuse', the ordinary owner will soon discover that to be an understatement, on a par with the advice that the coat 'if given a few minutes attention daily will give no trouble'. I recommend this remark to anyone who has been taken for a walk by a bobtail on a muddy day.

The tail is the only bit of him that gives no trouble. I have read somewhere, or have been told, that the bobtail owes his existence to a dog-tax, exemption from taxation being claimed for dogs with no tail worth speaking of. Whether this be factually true or not, it seems certain that some puppies around Langdale in Westmorland were born as tailless as cats on the Isle of Man, and that this freak of Nature was naturally encouraged in the interests of economy as well as convenience. It cannot, however, be depended upon, and a high percentage of puppies need to have their tails docked in the usual way a few days after birth.

The eyes, when you can see them, may be dark or wall-eyed, meaning that one of them is a mottled blue, which adds a quizzical touch to an otherwise serious person whose function in life is to help in herding sheep, a function he is reputed to perform by running over the backs of the flock as a short-cut to heading them off instead of running round them. But he can run round them too, for it is likewise reported that one poor Bobby so well obeyed the order his master forgot to cancel, that he kept going round and round until he dropped dead of exhaustion.

His ancestry is in dispute. He may have some affinity with a shaggy Russian animal called the Owtcher, or with the Russian pointer, or with the bearded collie whose portrait will be found facing page 129. Whatever his ancestry, and whatever the bother involved in keeping him reasonably un-matted and tidy, I think his charm is that throughout all his adult life he will continue to resemble an enormous puppy, rather like the playful one that pounced and frightened Alice in Wonderland in Sir John Tenniel's drawing.

Music-lovers may recall that that grand old eccentric Dame Ethel Smyth had a series of bobtails, all successively called Pan, Pan I, Pan II, up to Pan VII or possibly Pan VIII.

twenty-two

THE PEKINGESE

If the Pekingese is really the sleeve-dog of ancient China, it was well adapted for this method of transport, for this bundle of fur should not weigh more than something between seven and eleven pounds. Its smallness and softness belie the character of one who is in fact no luxury knick-knack, but as sporting as a terrier and as courageous as a little lion. Not that I ever want one for myself; I like large dogs.

They were much esteemed in the Imperial Palace, where, like the geese on the Roman Capitol, they could be relied on to give the alarm. Distinctions could be conferred on them by the reigning Emperor: one dog in the second century AD was accorded literary rank, and wore a hat nearly nine inches high at the front and three inches at the back, with a breadth of ten inches across. The same Emperor also ordained that the bitches should be regarded as the wives of officials, a most unpopular edict amongst the officials, and it is perhaps just as well that we should not know what the wives thought of it.

The edict in itself is enough to show in what ridiculously high honour the sleeve-dog was held. It might be compared with the mad wanton fantasy of the Roman emperor Caligula, who bestowed the rank of Consul on a favourite horse, loaded it with pearl-studded trappings, and stabled it in marble halls.

Even so late as 1893 the penalty for removing a dog from the Palace was death, and in earlier times the same punishment was inflicted for merely owning one, did the owner not happen to be of royal blood.

Very few of the sleeve-dogs found their way to Europe, though Buffon produces an unconvincing illustration in 1792. It was not until after the Boxer Rebellion in 1860, when five probably angry and frightened Pekes were found in a room of the deserted Palace beside the dead body of the Emperor's aunt, that the breed became established in England. These five were picked up by the British, and found suitably patrician homes in England, one of them being presented to Queen Victoria herself, two to the Duchess of Richmond, one to the Duchess of Wellington, and one being retained by a naval captain, the Duchess of Wellington's brother, Lord John Hay. By 1902 their numbers, thanks to a few additions, sometimes smuggled out of China, had increased sufficiently for them to be allotted a separate class by the Kennel Club. In 1900 there had been only one entry at Crufts.

If, as is considered desirable on the show-bench, the eyes should be 'large, dark, prominent, round, and lustrous', the specimen in the illustration certainly lives up to requirements. His eyes suggest mischievous headlamps which no motorist would like to encounter, undipped, along the road. But most owners of Pekes do not think in terms of the show-bench, nor even of motoring at night.

twenty-three

THE ALSATIAN

If I lived on a desert island, I should undoubtedly keep an Alsatian. Beautiful, noble, intelligent and devoted, they have only one fault: they bite.

I know that there has been a great deal of argument around this subject, but regretfully one must acknowledge facts. Alsatians are deeply suspicious of strangers and are apt to express their disapproval by the only means at their command. It is no good saying that this proceeds from an instinct laudably due to a desire to protect their owner: the inconvenient result remains. It is no good arguing either that the modern English-bred

Alsatian has no wolf-blood in him (although in 1887 the Germans were openly crossing wolves with dogs, and in fact advertised them as *Wolfs-hunde*), nor that any fresh wolf-strain has been introduced into our country. I know only too well the drawback of owning a dog that leaps at the wrist of anyone attempting to shake hands with you. Explanations and apologies avail little.

On the other hand, if you are so fortunate as to acquire an Alsatian of gentle temperament – and they do exist – no more perfect companion could be desired. A dog so sensitive as to tempt you to believe he can read your thoughts; so intelligent that he can be trained to anything from the simplest rules of obedience to the highly developed technique required of a Guide to the Blind; so handsome in appearance, with his pricked ears, golden eyes, deep ruff and thick soft coat – what more could one ask? I had such a dog once, and salute the memory of Rollo.

This may be the place to say something about guide dogs, for although Labradors, collies and retrievers are also used, the Alsatian tops the list. These wonderful guide dogs are first taught four essential words of command: Sit, Forward, Left, Right. Forward means: cross the road. But, if in the dog's judgment it is not safe to go forward, he must disobey the order his own master has given him. Now it is easy enough to teach a dog obedience, but to teach him *dis*obedience on his own initiative seems almost miraculous.

twenty-four

THE IRISH WATER SPANIEL

If ever a dog looked like a Restoration coffee-house character, this is he. Rather scruffy, out-at-elbows, and down-at-heel; a hanger-on of any rich patron he might pick up. Those mean, screwed-up eyes give evidence of a cynical outlook, the sad necessity of the failure in life to make the most of any chance that comes his way. One suspects his curls and ringlets, in imitation of the reigning monarch and his courtiers, of not being too clean. Altogether a disreputable ragamuffin, for whom one might feel compassion but not affection.

This conception of the Irish water spaniel is all wrong. Far from dating back to the days of the Restoration, no mention of him occurs until 1845, when he plunges into a rough sea to save the life of a boy, and subsequently endeavours to rescue a drunkard who dragged poor Bagsman under water with him when they were both drowned. This presents a very different picture from my imaginary wastrel haunting the low dens of Charles II's London. Of course, the absence of records before 1845 does not mean that he had not been splashing about in his peat bogs and going after duck in the marshes, long before that date. Indeed, two distinct varieties were presently recognised, the dogs from Northern Ireland being liver or liver and white, and the dogs from Southern Ireland invariably pure liver. (It is an odd fact that most Irish dogs come within the range of colour red to brown: the setter, the terrier, and the water spaniel. The Irish wolfhound, tallest dog in the world, not to be confused with the old Irish wolf dog now extinct, is usually grey or brindled, but then he is not Irish, if the Irish Guards whose mascot he is will forgive me for saying so. He is the result of a cross between the Scottish deerhound and the Great Dane.)

If the water spaniel can scarcely be called beautiful, he can at least be called useful and well-adapted to his function in life. That curly coat is oily, and a good shake throws off the water in a spray which his master would be well advised to evade. (There is probably something of the poodle in him, contributing to the tight curls.) Then there is his tail, not a thing of beauty either, but practical in so far as it is almost hairless and thus not liable by a sodden weight to impede its owner on his passage through the swamps. It is perhaps the ugliest tail any dog could be afflicted with. I would describe it as the tail of a nightmarish giant rat. Breeders call it 'stiff as a ramrod', and point out that he flourishes it whenever he scents game. It is difficult to imagine how a ramrod can be flourished, but one must accept their word for it. Personally, I feel sorry for the water spaniel in having such a repulsive object attached to his rump. Tails ought to be an ornament, bushy, friendly, and expressively waggy – not stiff as a ramrod. The water spaniel has had a poor deal.

twenty-five

THE FOXHOUND

It is seldom that one sees him by himself, a solitary specimen. There ought to be lots of him. Occasionally one meets him, anxious, muddy, trailing miserably down a ride, having mislaid the whole warrant of his existence, another twenty or thirty couple of his own kind, and somehow aware that he has not only missed the fun but has also managed to make a fool of himself.

Of all bloodsports, fox hunting is perhaps the least odious to the civilised mind. It cannot compete for wanton brutality with stag hunting, nor otter hunting. Foxes must be kept down, and it is no good getting sentimental about it. Some humanitarians say 'Shoot the fox', but country people know that for one fox cleanly shot dead, others will creep away wounded to die after days in the secrecy of the wood. No, what one dislikes about fox hunting is the attitude of people who indulge in it: 'Oh, the old scamp enjoys the run as much as anybody, y'know' – or, if they are facetiously minded, they may call the old scamp Charles James. If only they would be honest and say: 'Yes, we revel in the excitement of a good run; we think it a good thing to keep up the standard of our horses and the pluck of our young people; besides, the Hunt is a highly picturesque adjunct to our rural scene; we should be the poorer, deprived of it, and if the fox doesn't like it, so much the worse for him.' That would at least be truthful and respect-worthy. As it is, the hypocrisy which attends the whole business is as characteristically English as the picturesque adjunct to our rural scene – which I confess carries me out of my senses whenever it comes my way.

If any fox hunter boils up in rage against these remarks, let him reflect for a moment. Would he take equal pleasure in riding across country after a trail laid by a drag of aniseed? Of course he would not, because there would be no kill, or hope of a kill, at the end. Yes,

I know the argument about hounds working more interestingly on the scent of the living fox, doubling back, taking to water, doing all he can to preserve his life from his pursuers, but in the last resort it remains true that the primitive bloodlust shamefully lurks behind the whole beautiful traditional picturesque paraphernalia.

Deny it who can.

Oddly enough, we have very little information as to the origin of foxhounds and fox hunting. Edward I, in the years 1299 and 1300, kept twelve 'fox dogs', which are more likely to have been some kind of terrier than the foxhound as we know it. The first true pack of foxhounds may be claimed for Lord Lowther in 1666, when he took his pack down from Westmorland into what is now the Cottesmore country in Leicestershire and Rutland, or for a Mr T. Boothby who hunted Leicestershire for fifty five seasons, 1698–1753, with what is said to have been 'the first pack of foxhounds then in England'. These eighteenth-century packs are believed to have followed both the hare and the fox, and 'only gradually did it become the fashion to concentrate upon the latter'.

twenty-six

THE KERRY BLUE TERRIER

The Kerry Blue departs from the general rule of Irish dogs, by not being red or brown. In extreme youth he may try to adhere to it, for the puppies are sometimes stained with tan, but after a year or eighteen months these markings should all have disappeared. So do not be alarmed if your puppy apparently fails to conform to the rather pretty light silver, dark silver, or inky blue of his race.

Inky blue should be qualified. It may be like ink diluted with water, or it may be so dark a blue as to be almost blue-black.

I am afraid one must admit that his colouring is the only pretty thing about him. How would you like to be afflicted with such a beard, growing almost out of your eyes? Furthermore, show bench fashion decrees that the beard shall be clipped square; and this, combined with his straight legs, curly coat, and thin stick of an upright tail, gives him a wooden appearance more like a child's toy to be dragged on wheels than like any self-respecting dog. Yet this is perhaps not quite fair on the Kerry Blue. By all accounts, he is a very real dog, sporting by nature and capable of being trained as a retriever; a good ratter, and 'afraid of neither man nor beast'. This makes him a good guard dog, though at the same time he is said to be trustworthy with children and devoted to his owners. His coat, also, is soft to the touch, rather like a lamb.

twenty-seven

THE DACHSHUND

His business in life is to dig out badgers, *Dachs* being the German for badger, and dig he does, busily, even where there are no badgers. He will scrabble holes in the lawn and the flowerbeds, regardless of the gardener's feelings. His short front legs are as well adapted to such an occupation as his long nose to probe and snuffle. When not engaged on this mischief, he sits with his fat paws turned out in what dancing masters call the first position, for above all things he is neat and smooth and tidy.

He is a headstrong little dog, full of character. It is rather unfair on him that he should be regarded as a comic – the sausage dog, described in *Punch* as the kind of dog that is sold by the yard. His appearance may be on the comic side, lending itself to the caricaturists, but his personality is very much his own; and most idiosyncratic. No two dachshunds are quite alike. He is an amusing mixture of independence and dependence – out on his dig for the best part of the afternoon, and then coming in to demand affection in front of the teatime fire. For, like most Germans, he has his sentimental, cosy, bourgeois side. (It may be relevant to note that they were favourites of the Prince Consort.) I do not know whether the trait is common to all dachshunds, but the only two I have observed both entertained a deep devotion for another much larger dog, in one case a yellow Labrador, in the other case a black Pinscher. One has known dogs enjoying each other's company – it is much more fun, for instance, to hunt in couples than alone – but love which pines in separation is something more rare. These two small dachshunds both insist on sleeping in the arms of their big protectors, a sensible arrangement for the pair in chilly England; less so for the other two, whose home is in tropical Brazil. I should have thought it much too hot.

There are three types of coat: the smooth, the long-haired, and the wirehaired, and these three are repeated in the miniature version called by the Germans *Kaninchenteckel*, or rabbit dachshunds. I must say that the smooth-haired miniature reminds me more of a rat than of a rabbit; the late Major Lawrence Johnston of gardening fame had quite a pack of them, skinny little things with whiplash tails, wriggling in and out between one's ankles. I can imagine that it would be a nice dog to carry in a muff, if muffs were still in fashion: its tail would stick out at one end and its nose at the other, and its solid little body would be warm to the hands inside.

twenty-eight

THE ST BERNARD

How kind he looks, how kind he is! That great coat, those huge paws, those worried wrinkles as though he were wondering what he could do next to oblige, that massive frame which proclaims trustworthiness – this is the St Bernard, the friend. Even his puppy, in Messrs Hennessy's advertisement, already carries a miniature keg of brandy.

Legend clings about him. One would like to believe that some strange link connects him with the Tibetan mastiff, for, as some authorities have pointed out, there is a resemblance between the skulls of the Tibetan dog and the skulls found in a Romano-Helvetian settlement. Is this curious fact to be attributed to the geographical similarity between the Himalayan highlands and the Alps, both producing a huge breed which furthermore shares the unusual peculiarity of double dewclaws on the foreleg? Or did the Tibetan find his way across Asia to Switzerland in Roman times? I must confess that this strikes me as extremely unlikely.

One would also like to believe that his ancestors may have been found roaming wild over the mountains when the Hospice was founded by St Bernard de Menthon in the tenth century, but another theory propounds that the monks did not keep dogs until after 1800, a theory based on the admittedly negative evidence that travellers who have left descriptions of the Hospice before that date make no reference to any dogs at all. Notably in the *Dictionary of Switzerland*, 1788, which contains an account of the Hospice, the dogs are not mentioned, and similar instances could be quoted. By 1827 we have an account of large fawn-coloured dogs who accompanied the monks on their excursions, carrying bread, a small barrel of wine, and clothing tied round their necks; and subsequently the travellers' references multiply. It is certainly suggestive that earlier visitors should have remained silent.

The introduction of the St Bernard to this country was received with mixed feelings. One learned Judge gave it as his opinion that dogs of this size were all very well on the tops of mountains, but should not be allowed to run about the streets indulging in horseplay and knocking people down. One fanatically enthusiastic owner (a clergyman), however, took a very different view, and seriously discussed with Mr Gladstone 'whether or not the St Bernard dog had been put on earth by the Almighty solely for the purpose of saving life'. Certainly the life-saving legend dies hard, in spite of the protest sent home from the Hospice in 1887 by an English visitor, that 'some people think the dogs are occupied throughout the winter in grubbing in snowdrifts for lost travellers and pouring cognac down their throats when found ... His regular duty is rather to prevent the traveller from falling into danger than to save him from its consequences.'

It is a pathetic truth, recorded by the same visitor, that in the exercise of this duty the Hospice dogs suffer severely from the rheumatism they contract even during their first winter.

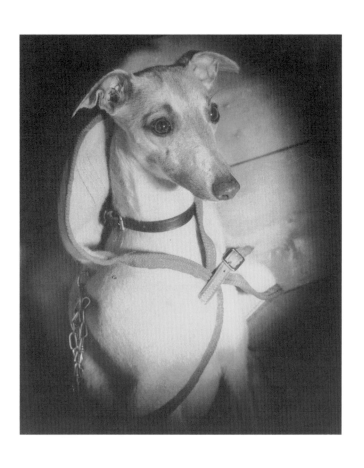

twenty-nine

THE WHIPPET

He is often mistaken for an Italian greyhound, but although roughly the same size he is, in fact, bred down from a greyhound by using terriers, but this does not prevent his being sometimes mistakenly called the Hitalian. He is *par excellence* the miner's dog, especially in Lancashire, Staffordshire and Durham. Miners seem to have a predilection for dogs of excessive refinement: witness the Yorkshire terrier, whose portrait with commentary will be found on p. 48. It must give them some queer twist of pleasure to handle something so utterly contrasted with their usual occupation of heaving huge heavy dirty lumps of coal about.

Not that the whippet is a luxury pet like the Yorkshire terrier. He does not have a topknot tied up with a bow of ribbon like a dog on the lid of a presentation chocolate box. He has no topknot, for he is sleek all over, nor does he lie in silken dalliance on a cushion, for he is above all things a sportsman, the central figure in that rough world of betting and sweepstakes, racing in 'lanes' on grass or cinder tracks, rabbit coursing, competition and rivalry. His racing speed is renowned, though unlike Dr Roger Bannister and Mr Christopher Chataway he does not aspire to the mile, but contents himself with short bursts conformable with his delicate nervous build and the sensibility of his disposition.

He is of an elegance that suggests an *objet d'art* rather than a high-mettled sporting creature. He should be carved in ivory. Stroke him, and you are almost surprised to feel a living warmth under the skin that covers those tiny bones. His legs in their frailty would arouse the envy of any American woman justifiably proud of her slender ankles: they look as though they might splinter at any moment. Yet they don't. The whippet can run! He is more exacting than the greyhound. Either he insists on having a real live rabbit to pursue, or else he will race his colleagues for the fun and excitement of it.

thirty

THE IRISH SETTER

The lean red dog is surely one of the most decorative of all the tribe. Never having owned one myself, I cannot speak personally for his character, though he is said to be gentle and intelligent and of his qualities as a gundog there can be no question. To me he always suggests a dog in a painting by Marcus Stone, somewhat sentimental, somewhat meditative, patiently waiting until his young master shall have finished his courtship of the muslin-frocked maiden in an English garden on a summer evening. I don't know if such a painting exists, but that is where he ought to be.

The setter is supposed to derive from a cross between spaniels and pointers, possibly in the seventeenth century and certainly before the end of the eighteenth. The Irish setter in particular appears to have resulted from a cross between a red spaniel and a Spanish pointer, which at first produced a medley of colours, red and white, pure white, pure black, or red with white or black patches, all indicating a throwback to the red and white or sometimes black Spanish pointer. The rich, glossy, red self colour now seems to be established, though a streak of white on the nose and some white on the chest or the feet does not disqualify on the show bench.

Mr Edward Ash has an interesting explanation of how the characteristics of the pointer and the spaniel were combined in the setter. Guns, he says, used to be clumsy weapons, slow to load, and it was therefore desirable for the sportsman to employ a dog which, on scenting game, would not pursue and flush it, but would remain stock-still, pointing, as though petrified or turned to stone, perhaps even with one paw lifted and arrested in mid-air – in other words, indicating to his master where it was likely to rise or run. The spaniel, on the other hand, could be trained to sit and remain sitting until called off; this accomplishment was especially valuable when game was to be driven into nets. Then, as guns became handier and birds could be more readily shot on the wing, the inherited qualities of pointer and spaniel came to be combined in the setter, a dog who would discover the presence of game and yet not rush after it, perhaps at too great a distance for an accurate discharge.

However this may be, I have often thought I would like to see a couple of these creatures draping them-selves in graceful attitudes on a flight of steps of Tudor brickwork, whose colour they would so suitably match.

thirty-one

THE CORGI

I have never known a corgi, and I am not sure that I want to. I have an idea that they are better employed as cattle herders on their native hills of Wales, than as bad-tempered pets in the home, or, as one writer less bluntly puts it, 'inclined to be a wee bit neurotic in temperament'. Perhaps I malign them and my limited experience may have been unfortunate; I know only that when corgi owners bring their darlings into my garden, they invariably quarrel with my friendly little Border collie who is full of hospitable instincts and wants to make his guests welcome, instead of getting bitten on the nose and his coat savaged.

The photograph shows him in an unamiable light, not as the docile minion one sees leaving for Balmoral or Sandringham with the other end of his lead in some royal hand. I find his appearance attractive, so stocky and alert. There are two varieties recognised by the Kennel Club: the Cardigan and the Pembroke, the difference being that the Cardigan has a tail and the Pembroke no tail to speak of. This seems a curiously arbitrary distinction, as very few puppies are born with a stumpy tail and the effect is artificially produced by docking; a more justifiable reason would appear to be that the Pembroke stands lower to the ground on shorter legs.

I wish by the way that I knew why some writers on dogs find it necessary to refer to tails as 'caudal appendages'. What is wrong with tail?

The Pembroke is far and away the more popular variety. It is certainly the neater and more compact of the two, but personally I prefer the less truncated look of the Cardigan. Their name? It derives from *gi* or *ci*, a dog; and *cor*, a dwarf.

thirty-two

THE CHIHUAHUA

People who favour very small things could scarcely do better than acquire a Mexican fairy dog or Chihuahua, for a prize specimen may weigh no more than 2 lb, and I should imagine that a puppy might be mistaken for a mouse. They are thus eminently portable and transportable, though it is said that they will allow no one but their owner to pick them up. Can this characteristic relate to some atavistic instinct of self protection, some lingering memory of the days when Aztec priests laid them on sacrificial altars, and the gourmets of Mexico ate them, much as we today should eat quail or ortolan?

Yet at the same time they were sometimes called royal dogs, because the Emperor Montezuma gave a couple of the gay little creatures to his daughter. The Spaniards noticed them during their conquest of Mexico, and an unconfirmed legend suggests that they brought some back to Spain. Be that as it may, it is certain that the Chihuahua did not find its way to Britain until quite recently.

Extremely pert, with their tulip or butterfly ears and Shakespearian domed foreheads, they are amusing in appearance and merry in disposition. They must not be confused with the Mexican hairless dog, a freak of which I know nothing except that I have no desire to see one, let alone own one. I would as soon own a rat. Nor do I really want a Chihuahua, although a friend of mine assures me that you could not have a more diverting companion. I will take her word for it, and leave it at that.

Their name may sound odd and even unpronounce-able to our British ears, which is only to be expected when it comes from that far-away country, rent by earth-quakes, explosive with volcanoes, bloodstained in history, and with a language far removed from any Western or Aryan tongue. The name is pronounced, more or less, She-wha-wha, and derives from the town Chihuahua, capital of the eponymous district rich in silver mines, some thousand miles north of Mexico City. Don't ask me what Chihuahua means, for I do not know.

thirty-three

THE BEARDED COLLIE

You would not take him for a collie, would you, if by a collie you mean something with a pointed nose? But if under the name collie you include all kinds of sheepdog, then he must qualify, even as the old bobtail qualifies. This large moon-faced amiable fluffy-faced creature looks more like an old bobtail whose mother had made a mésalliance with a hearth-rug, than like the elegant little Sheltie or even than the Welsh and Border collies who perform so brilliantly at the sheepdog trials.

He is the 'big rough towsie-looking tyke' of Highland shepherds, and I am sorry to say that very few of them appear in the Kennel Club list of registrations.

Yet am I really sorry?

Is it not rather pleasant in these days of popularisation and advertisement, to reflect that somewhere in the still romantic North of these islands the Scottish shepherd privately tramps the hills with his dog at heel or ranging at command, and no thought of registration with an unknown organisation in London?

How greatly I prefer this proud reticence to the glossy-magazine fashionable miniature poodle who tops the list.

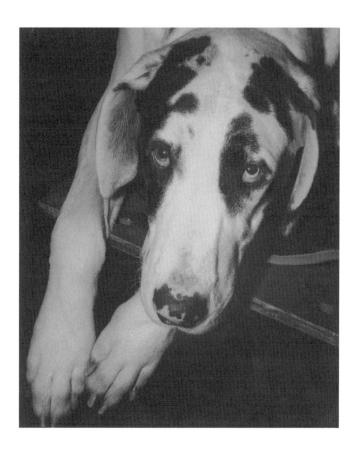

thirty-four

THE GREAT DANE

Unlike the Dalmatian, the Great Dane may well come from the country which gives him his name, though he has also been claimed by Germany. This hugely alarming dog, like many large men, usually has the kindliest disposition; I feel sure he enjoyed carrying a lamp in his mouth ahead of benighted travellers, by his mere presence assuring them of their safety, as he was taught to do in the eighteenth century. He could also be sent back five or six miles to retrieve a forgotten parcel. These were among the services he was pleased to render.

It seems scarcely necessary to say that he should be wisely handled from puppyhood, for an undisciplined or irritable Great Dane is a terrifying thought. Even an amiable one, anxious to please, provides some elements of peril. Too exuberant a display of affection will easily land you on the floor, and there is also the tail to be considered. It is long, and as hard as a piece of wood, and unlike a piece of wood it wags. Now this tail may get damaged if the dog is confined in too small a kennel, and so generally is this danger recognised that dog shops supply a special tail-protector. In my admittedly limited experience of the breed, I have noticed that danger *from* the tail is as much to be taken into account as danger *to* the tail. One happy swoop across a low table, and off go all the tea cups.

Dear Brutus! The only Great Dane I ever intimately knew. How remorseful he was whenever his enormous clumsiness had led him into transgression. He seemed to say he knew he had done wrong, but how could he help it? His owner, the poet Dorothy Wellesley, forgave him all his trespasses:

> My great marbled hound (she wrote)
> Leaps at them (the rooks) as they fly.

The one in the illustration is a harlequin, which means that he may have a wall-eye and a pink nose. This truly noble dog, this great marbled hound, ought to be seen in his entirety. He stands 30 inches tall, and weighs at the minimum 120 lb or nearly ten stone. He has been with us for some two hundred years, possibly three hundred, when dogs were used for pulling carts, even as they are used today in Belgium and Holland. So muscular a dog as the Dane, almost the size of a Shetland pony, would have been well adapted to cart harness. Why not use him today, to pull the mowing machine?

thirty-five

THE PAPILLON OR
BUTTERFLY-DOG

He gets his nickname from his ears, which do in some way resemble the open wings of a butterfly, although no butterfly ever sported such richly fringed hairy wings. The first shower of rain would soon bring it down if it did. Even the Butterfly-dog does not always hold his ears upright, but sometimes allows them to droop. When they droop, he is known as the *Epagneul nain*, dwarf Spaniel, or the Toy Spaniel of Bologna, who was carried in crates on mule-back from Bologna to Paris on the order of Louis XIV.

He is very small and light. The ideal weight is between 3 and 6 lb, but the smaller the better. He has a very profuse silky coat, a heavily fringed tail, which curls over the back like the tail of a red squirrel, and large, round, dark eyes which can be seen to advantage in the illustration. He is well described as 'a luxury dog, a pretty little thing', and one can readily imagine the ladies of Louis's highly artificial Court taking him into favour as an adjunct to their silks and satins. Besides, he seems to have been associated with the Comforter, or Spaniel-Gentle who could be rubbed up and down against the abdomen or chest of a sick person to relieve indigestion or fever. This must be a very old tradition, persisting from the fifteenth century right up to 1790, when the Papillon is credited by Thomas Bewick with similar powers.

The Butterfly-dog may, dubiously, be related to the Chihuahua of Mexico, to whom he bears a certain resemblance, especially about the ears. But as the importation of the Chihuahua into Europe by the Spaniards must remain in doubt until further evidence comes to light, the Papillon must remain what he is now considered – a Belgian who made his entry into England only in 1922.

He is usually tricoloured but can be white with patches of brown, but never wholly self-coloured.

thirty-six

THE BULLDOG

The soft-hearted, or even the averagely humane, are not advised to read descriptions of battles between bulls and bulldogs. The horror and brutality of such encounters make one ask oneself how the English in their self-righteousness can ever dare to criticise the Spanish bullfight. There are stories of the bull, who anyhow was usually tethered to a stake and thus given no fair chance to defend himself, having his hooves chopped off by an axe, and left to continue the fight on four raw stumps; stories of boiling water poured into his ears to enliven him when he showed signs of exhaustion; and, even more shocking as a revelation of human heartlessness and cupidity, stories of owners hacking the feet off their own dogs while hanging on to the bull's nostrils and not letting go, to prove their valour and obtain a higher price for their progeny.

No wonder Samuel Pepys considered bullbaiting 'a very rude and nasty pleasure'. But he was in advance of his times.

It was not until 1853 that bullbaiting was abolished by Act of Parliament in this country. Several attempts had already been made, but had been defeated on the plea that 'the pluck of the English nation would certainly decrease if the Bill became Law', and also that the Bill was a conspiracy on the part of Jacobins and Methodists to 'make life dull'.

It is pleasing to find Richard Brinsley Sheridan, in 1802, speaking in the House of Commons in favour of the abolition. One likes to think of intellectuals being on the enlightened side of the angels.

Even after the Bill had finally been carried, fights between dogs were still countenanced for some years, but, however bloody, the protagonists were at least better matched and probably enjoyed a set-to with one of their own kind and size. Nothing will stop dogs, like small boys, from being quarrelsome, whatever may be the hope for the future of adult mankind. It appears, however, that the bulldog is really quite a gentle creature in private life: it is his formidable aspect which has gained him his reputation. As a Staffordshire farmer once remarked, two bulldogs loose in his yard did more to make his neighbours honest than all the parson's preaching.

To conclude, I do not think we can say that the pluck of the English nation has decreased much since the Bill of 1853 became Law.

thirty-seven

THE SHIH TZU

I have always understood that Tibet was one of the windiest countries in the world, eternal gales raging across gritty plains, yet by some oversight of Nature the dogs of Tibet, with the exception of the Tibetan mastiff, have all been created so small that you would expect them to be blown away. Ten inches of fur is not much to stand up against a hurricane. At least they have been well provided with thick coats and plenty of courage, and it seems also that Tibetan bitches have evolved a most ingenious biological arrangement by which they come into season only once a year. How wise of them, considering the horrible conditions they have to endure.

The small object (I really cannot call it anything else) in the illustration is sometimes known as the Tibetan lion-dog because of its bravery; in fact I am given to understand that Shih Tzu (pronounced Shid-zoo) means lion in Chinese. It looks to me more like a dog for the boudoir with a bow of ribbon in its topknot than for the rigours of its native climate. But a photograph of the whole beastie would show how low it stands to the ground, how four-square, on the chubbiest of short legs, with its tail curled well over its back in a general attitude of determination and even defiance.

Besides the Shih Tzu we have the Tibetan spaniel, the Lhasa terrier, and the Lhasa Apso. The spaniel looks alert, pert, and attractive, with butterfly ears, and for the life of me I cannot see the proclaimed resemblance to the Pekingese, whose ancestor it is sometimes supposed to be. It has a sharp nose, not a squashed nose. The Lhasa terrier looks a mess, like a very diminutive edition of the Old English sheepdog seen through the wrong end of opera-glasses. They have their uses, for their long hair may be shorn and woven into clothing. The Lhasa Apso is perhaps the aristocrat among Tibetan dogs, for he was bred in the palace of the Dalai Lama and in the monasteries. I found him described as 'a very intellectual little creature', whatever that may mean.

It should go without saying that none of these breeds has been long in this country, for Tibet was for many centuries an almost unknown land, with Lhasa itself a forbidden city.

thirty-eight

THE LABRADOR RETRIEVER

Dear, solid, faithful lump of a dog! The only one I ever intimately knew was called True, and never was dog more rightly named. You could not claim that he was brilliantly clever (though by no means stupid), but he was utterly dependable and invariable in his character. You could shove him around – 'Get out of my way, True' – and all he would do would be to grunt in a language of his own, rather grumpy, but deeply affectionate, and rather apologetic for having got his massive body in your way without meaning to.

He was (and I rejoice to say still is, for this is not an obituary notice) a golden coloured Labrador. Two colours are usual: the yellow and the black. True had chosen the golden. He had never been trained as a gundog, but waddled contentedly around as a family-friend, rather like a pensioned-off Nannie with a thickening waistline, slightly disapproving of the antics of the younger generation but still determined to protect his home and its inhabitants from any outside interference. Growl; grouse; grumble; grunt. 'Where's my dinner? Hope it's not been forgotten. Things aren't what they were. Must look after my people all the same. Must see to it that gypsies don't steal the daffodils out of their orchard at night . . .'

The only thing he does, in what might be called a retrieving way, is to collect hedgehogs. Hedgehogs seem to be becoming rare nowadays, but True finds them, picks them up, and deposits them with the utmost delicacy at the back door.

So he trundles round, protective old Nannie, grousing away at all the things he disapproves of. He now has a new young love to fill his ageing life. This is a dachshund, who most touchingly nestles up against him and sleeps against the warmth of True's heavy body, embraced by True's kind arms.

It must seem, to True, like having a new baby to look after.

How very different from the prickly hedgehogs that True so cleverly collects, without getting stabbed by the prickles.

thirty-nine

THE MONGREL

Alas, we can honour him with no history, no pedigree. He must speak for himself, with those great wistful eyes, as appealing as a lost child. Fortunately for him he is well able to do so. I have owned, or been owned by, several mongrels in my time, and never have I known dogs more capable of falling on their feet. Some of them have been pi-dogs; one made her way into my house in Constantinople, and, too savage to be ejected, gave birth to a litter of puppies on the drawing-room sofa; another dreadful little object collected me in the bazaars of Teheran, followed me home, and took complete possession. The faces of the Persian servants when I made them give him a bath, badly needed, were worth seeing.

Then there was Micky, who had a dash of Irish terrier in him. I think Micky must be the only dog who has openly walked ashore off a battleship on to English soil without being intercepted and clapped into quarantine. I had left him behind in Turkey, when, unable to return myself owing to the outbreak of war, the Ambassador who detested dogs but to whom I remain eternally grateful brought him home to me on a string. Micky it was, too, who, falling through a skylight when he ought by all the rules to have been killed, contrived to land on a bed – though that was perhaps due to good luck rather than to good management.

The worst of mongrels is that they are apt to be so very plain. Micky himself was no beauty. Good breeding tells. One has noticed the extreme ungainliness of dogs lying about the streets of foreign villages, and has been thankful that the proportion of these mistakes is not so high in Britain. But for sheer urchin wit and resourcefulness the mongrel can be hard to beat, only unfortunately when tempted to acquire an irresistible puppy one is seldom aware of its lineage, immediate or remote, and thus cannot estimate what characteristics it is likely to develop in later life. Will it have a bit of the sheepdog in it, and proudly but inconveniently bring one a flock of sheep belonging to somebody else? Will it have a bit of terrier, and have to be dragged backwards by the tail out of a rabbit-hole? Or will it be merely a small scavenger, preferring unspeakable filth to the nice bowl we painstakingly provide? One must take one's chance, and in most cases one's life is no longer likely to be one's own.

forty

THE BASENJI

There can be no doubt of the intelligence revealed in that face, and from all I hear of the Basenji he should find increasing favour as he becomes better known. He had never been seen in England until 1937, when a Mrs Burn brought him from the Kwango district on a tributary of the Congo, where the natives employed him in tracking wounded game. He is not inconveniently large, standing 16 to 18 inches at the shoulder, and in spite of his country of origin he is said to adapt himself quite happily to our very different climate, and even grows a thicker coat during the winter.

In colour he is usually a rich chestnut, like a conker, with a white tip to his tightly curled tail, though sometimes he is black-and-white, or black, brown, and white; sometimes tiger-striped red with black stripes; occasionally cream-coloured, which for some reason is condemned by show-bench judges. He has certain amusing peculiarities: a remarkably loose skin which you can pick up in handfuls along his back and which enables him to wrinkle his forehead in moments of excitement, and, oddest of all, *he never barks*. I must say that I long to meet a Basenji and hear his substitute for a bark, which is described as 'a pleasant yodel, not unlike a young cockerel's first attempts at crowing'. I wonder what the nocturnal burglar would make of it?

As to his personal character, I cannot do better than quote from Miss Veronica Tudor-Williams, herself a breeder who has travelled to Africa in search of Basenjis. After describing its impish ways, almost uncanny sense of fun, she says: 'No dog has brought apology to a finer art. How can one be cross with an animal which lies on its back with both hands folded over its eyes, or stands on its head turning somersaults, or peeps round the door watching the reactions of an indignant owner, yodelling loudly when it finds the moment of retribution can no longer be averted?'

Although a newcomer to Europe, a very ancient ancestry is claimed for him, no doubt with some justification if he has traditionally been used by the tribes of Central Africa for many centuries in the past. Moreover, his portrait or anyhow something remarkably like it appears in carvings on Egyptian tombs, circa 1200 BC, sitting beside his master, complete with collar, lead, and bell attached to the collar. The bell was provided because, the dog being barkless, its tinkle gave an indication as to his whereabouts in the undergrowth. It is interesting to find that the tribes of Central Africa still carry on the same practical idea that occurred to the Egyptians all that long time ago.

The African owners will not readily part with their dogs. They will not sell them for even a double or treble price of a bride nor even for bribes of jewellery or cigarettes. I like them for that. Basenji apparently means a bush thing, or a wild thing, and I like to feel that there are still some wild things left in this over-civilised world.

forty-one

THE COLLIE

There are, roughly speaking, five types of collie: the rough and the smooth, which are large; the Welsh and the Border, which are small; and the Shetland or Sheltie, which is smallest of all. The smooth-coated collie has never been so popular as the rough; some shepherds may have found short coats more convenient in wet weather, but the rough is incomparably the more beautiful animal, with its silky coat, the frill, the gentle expression, the graceful build, the intelligence in those watchful eyes.

His honest, sonsie, bawsent face
Aye got him friends in ilka place.

There is also the bearded collie, whose portrait is facing page 129.

All collies are extremely sensitive, which may account for their reputation for a treacherous temper. If offended or frightened, they retaliate. The reverse of the medal is their excessive devotion. Who has not shed a tear for Owd Bob in fiction, or over the recent real-life story of the dog who stayed for three months by the dead body of his shepherd, lost on the snow-bound moors?

Ideally the collie should be a working dog; he should follow his natural profession. Thwarted of this, his hereditary instinct is still predominant, sometimes in amusing ways. My own Border collie, because as a puppy he was never employed in herding sheep, still tries to herd the clumps of daffodils in the orchard, running round them in circles and snapping with exasperation when he cannot get them to move. More regrettably, he also tries to herd people into groups, and is not above giving a nip to the human ankle as he would nip at the fetlock of a recalcitrant sheep. When one thinks of the almost incredible sagacity displayed at the sheepdog trials, it seems wasteful to turn such marvellous material into a mere pet.

These little cattle-herders, apart from their peculiar aptitude for driving sheep through hurdles where sheep don't want to go, have many pretty and endearing ways. I have never known any other dog who would sit hanging his head, in expectation of a scolding. Puzzling and idiosyncratic companions, I have come to the conclusion that they are a bit fey. It must be due to the Celtic strain in them.

How much one wishes, sometimes, that one's dog could explain what is going on inside his head; and that he could tell one how often in spite of all one's love, one misunderstands him.

forty-two

THE WIRE-HAIRED
FOX-TERRIER

Would it be heresy to suggest that this workmanlike little dog is really rather ugly? The fashion for trimming his beard square, above his absolutely straight forelegs, results in making him look as though he were carved out of a block of wood. The one in the photograph has evidently not been intended for the show-bench and has escaped the trimmer's attentions; he was probably just someone's jolly companion, who barked when strangers came, bit the postman, and kept the rats down.

Both kinds of fox-terrier, the smooth and the wire-haired, descend from the Old British black-and-tan, now extinct except in its miniature form, jet-black and shiny, with rust-red markings, and weighing anything from 3 to 8 lb. They are thus unquestionably English dogs, though their name of terrier comes from the French, *terre*, earth, indicating that they readily go to earth, i.e. down holes or drains, in pursuit of their prey. The first fox-terriers were nearly all smooth-coated, and were probably shorter in the leg than the modern dog; in the reign of James I some of them were crooked-legged as well, a thing which would never be tolerated today.

Until the second half of the nineteenth century the wiry coat occurred more or less as a freak, though some time in the 1870s an Oxford undergraduate named John Russell meditatively strolling across Magdalen meadow met a milkman accompanied by a small wire-haired bitch. She took his fancy and he bought her, to become the matriarch of the now well-known Russell terriers.

It was not until about twenty years later that the few wire-haired dogs which occasionally appeared ceased to be described as 'objectionable', and started to make headway and even to command high prices, until today they have outstripped their smooth-coated kindred in numbers and popularity.

Fox-terriers will always be liked. They are cheerful, companionable, and sporting. Essentially normal, hearty dogs, with no Freudian neurotic nonsense about them, they seem to have been created as the born friend of the country-born Englishman or Englishwoman. They go well with tweed suits and brogue shoes. Yes, they are very English: what Kipling might have called a Man's Pal.

forty-three

THE MASTIFF

Buffon called the mastiff, quite simply, *Le Dogue*, thus conforming to the common belief that the breed was British. This was not strictly accurate, for mastiffs were known to the Babylonians, the Assyrians, the Egyptians, the Greeks, and to the Romans against whom they were used in tribal wars, fighting in packs, encased in armour. It is however true that the Romans found them already established in Britain, savage animals, to whom they gave the name *canis pugnaces*, and whom they imported to Rome for use in the arena. They appear also on the Bayeux Tapestry, accompanying Harold on his way to Bosham.

Pugnaces indeed, the poor mastiff became subject to legal control; in other words, he was deliberately lamed in order to deter him from the pursuit of deer and other game, especially in the royal forests. Either the pad was cut out, or else three toes were chopped off with an axe. Let us turn from this revolting practice to a more picturesque story, when in 1614 King James I sent four mastiffs as a gift to the Great Mogul, in the care of the East India Company.

Only two of them survived the journey, one of them having been lost overboard when he leapt into the sea on perceiving a shoal of porpoises. The remaining two, wearing heavy silver collars, on arrival in India, were put into kennels disguised as little coaches, gaily painted and mounted on painted wheels. Native boys drew the coaches, and other boys trotted alongside, fanning the occupants. So well pleased was the Mogul, that he allotted four attendants to each dog, two to carry them up and down in palanquins and two to fan and keep the flies off them.

Like the bulldog, mastiffs were used for baiting bulls, bears and even lions. Four of these 'vast, huge, stubborn, eager' dogs would be set against a lion in the time of Queen Elizabeth I; three were considered sufficient to tackle a bear. (One of the Great Mogul's dogs took on an elephant single-handed.) The mastiff was also used as a guard-dog, when it was sensibly stipulated that he should be 'no gadder abroad, nor lavishe of his mouth, barking without cause', a recommendation which might be followed with advantage by some straying, yapping terriers one has known.

The mastiff is perhaps not everybody's pet. He eats too much. What else can you expect of a creature that weighs ten stone? His numbers diminished seriously with war-rationing; dog-of-war at some stages in history, he was not an easy guest in modern war. I hope his numbers will build up again, for it would be a pity to lose the magnificent animal that defended our forefathers against the Roman invader.

forty-four

THE SAMOYED

The photograph is somewhat misleading, for the foreshortening does not suggest the sharp, pointed nose and alert expression of this beautiful dog. It does suggest the soft depths of the snowy fur, into which one is tempted to plunge one's hands, as much for the pleasure of touch as for warmth. The mind recoils before the thought of this coat shorn, leaving its owner looking as ungainly as a freshly shorn sheep, but that is what happens or used to happen in the cold Siberian north, the grim country he inhabits, where the fur was woven into clothes and blankets.

There is something very gallant and attractive about all these deepcoated, prick-eared, curly-tailed dogs – the Samoyed, the elk-hound, and the keeshond. They look ready for anything, as might be expected, for their instinct is to serve. The Samoyed strains against his harness to pull the sledge and has in fact taken part like the husky in Arctic and Antarctic expeditions. Both he and the elk-hound are associated with that fairy-tale animal the reindeer, rounding up the herds in Siberia and Norway respectively. The smaller keeshond pulls carts for the Dutch and the Belgians, when he is not busy running up and down the decks of barges on the Dutch canals. But neither the grey elk-hound nor the grey barge-dog can boast that pure and dazzling coat of the Samoyed.

I had an elk-hound once (this is a digression) who, although quite fond of me in a patronising sort of way, was the most independent dog I ever knew. Nothing would induce that dog to stop at home, and whenever he got bored which was about once a week he used to walk up to the village, climb into the local bus, and get himself transported to a town some three miles away, where he would quarter himself on friends for a couple of days. Then he would come back, also by bus, unless he happened to see my car, when he would walk out in the middle of the road, stop me, and wait till I let him in. He had another habit of attending church services, when he would lie looking very handsome and perfectly quiet on the chancel steps; I don't think anybody ever attempted to remove him, for I must confess that, although irreproachably good-tempered, he was the terror of the villagers from whom he used to steal the food off their kitchen tables. But perhaps I have said enough about Canute the elk-hound in a note which really ought to have been concerned with his cousin the Samoyed.

Daunt Books

Founded in 2010, the Daunt Books imprint is dedicated to discovering brilliant works by talented authors from around the world. Whether reissuing beautiful new editions of lost classics or introducing fresh literary voices, we're drawn to writing that evokes a strong sense of place – novels, short fiction, memoirs, travel accounts, and translations with a lingering atmosphere, a thrilling story, and a distinctive style. With our roots as a travel bookshop, the titles we publish are inspired by the Daunt shops themselves, and the exciting atmosphere of discovery to be found in a good bookshop.

For more information, please visit
www.dauntbookspublishing.co.uk